Star Struck

Hip Hop

by Cathy West

Ransom

StarStruck

Hip Hop
by Cathy West

Illustrated by Demitri Nezis

Published by Ransom Publishing Ltd.
Radley House, 8 St. Cross Road, Winchester, Hants. SO23 9HX
www.ransom.co.uk

ISBN   978 184167 053 9
First published in 2014

Hip Hop

Contents

3

All About
Hip Hop

What is hip hop?

At first, hip hop was a way to make music. DJs used turntables and mixers to make new music from other records.

Rap was a new way of singing over this new music.

Now hip hop is more than just music.

It includes poetry and dance, as well as fashion and art.

People began to make art to go with the music. They used spray cans and made graffiti.

Where did hip hop start?

Hip hop started in New York, in the USA.

It all started in this building. In 1973 DJ Kool Herc was living here. At a party he started rapping and mixing using turntables.

It was the beginning of hip hop!

This is one of the first hip hop bands: Grandmaster Flash and the Furious Five.

In 1982 they had the first huge hip hop hit - The Message.

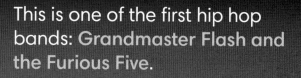

The Message was in the U.S. 'Hot 100' charts for 62 weeks.

Hip hop dance

Dance is a big part of hip hop. Hip hop has many kinds of dance styles.

Popping

When a dancer pops, they jerk their body quickly.

The movements they make are called pops, or hits.

Locking

When a dancer freezes in one position, it's called a lock.

Breaking

Sometimes called breakdancing.

Freeze

A **pose**, when you stop, or hold your position.

Jerking

Moving your legs in and out (that's called the **jerk**). Other moves are the **reject**, **dip** and **pindrop**.

Jooking

Popping, waving and **gliding** on your toes. It's harder than it looks!

11

Rap

Singing or speaking a fast rhyme over the music. The rhythm is important.

Sometimes the rapper is called the MC (or emcee).

Singer and rapper Kanye West.

Alternative hip hop

When hip hop is mixed with other kinds of music.

Kanye West is a well-known alternative hip hop star. He has sold over 87 million records.

12

Scratching, DJing

Using turntables and a mixer to move records forwards and backwards to a beat.

Rapper Angel Haze.

Now there a many different kinds of hip hop. How many of these do you know?

Freestyle	Ragga	Jazz rap
G-funk	Breakbeat	Chap hop.

Hip hop: get the look

Get the look! To be a hip hop star, you need to look like a hip hop star!

Fashions keep changing. So keep up to date. This is a good look:

 Baggy clothes

 Lots of bling

 Cool hairstyles

 Snapback hats are popular too.

You need a good name, too.

Snoop Dogg's real name is Calvin Cordozar Broadus, Jr.

Snoop Dogg is better!

But now he has changed his name to Snoop Lion.

Remember – you don't need to spend a lot to get the look.

Be creative! Make sure you show *your* personality as well.

15

How to be a great rapper

So you want to be a **great rapper**? Here's how!

 Listen to other rappers. Watch how they **perform**. Learn from what they do.

 Listen to the **beat**. Rap to the **beat**.

 Speak clearly and don't rush. People want to hear what you say.

 Practise! Then practise some more.

 Form a **hip hop group** with your friends.

 Try to play in front of an **audience**. Your friends and family are a good place to start.

Remember - write about what you *feel*.

It's *your* music! Don't pretend to be somebody else.

Singer and rapper **M.I.A.** She mixes hip hop with other kinds of music.

Chapter One

An awful noise

Malik and his band were singing one of the hip hop songs they had written.

His sister Tara came in to the room. She had her hands over her ears.

'What's that awful noise?' Tara asked.

'What do you know?' Malik snapped back. 'You don't know anything about hip hop!'

'I think we're really good,' said Malik. 'We're going to hire a hall and charge people to come and see us perform.'

Tara laughed.

'No one's going to pay to hear an unknown band,' she said. 'No matter how good *you* think you are.'

'Tara, you've got no idea about the music industry,' Malik said, shaking his head.

Chapter Two

Getting a gig

'You should do a free gig for the local youth club,' Tara told Malik.

'How would we make any money doing that?' Malik sneered.

'You'd get a name for yourself. I'll even make a video of the gig to put on YouTube. Then you'll be known world-wide.'

Malik nodded. It was a good idea.

Malik went to talk to the local youth club leader.

'Could our hip hop band perform here one evening?' he asked.

The youth club leader checked the club's calendar.

'You're in luck,' she said. 'There's a cancellation next Monday. You can play then.'

Chapter Three

'They're awful!'

On the night of the gig, Tara came along to record them.

The band started singing.

'Oh no! They're really bad!' the youth club leader said.

Tara looked around the hall. Everyone was covering their ears. Malik and the band didn't seem to notice.

The next day, Tara watched her video recording.

She had to agree with the youth club leader. Her brother and his hip hop band were really awful!

'I can't upload this to YouTube. They're rubbish,' she thought.

But Tara didn't want to tell her brother that the band were no good.

Instead, she used her laptop to remix their songs. When she was happy with them, she uploaded them to YouTube.

Chapter Four

The big day

A few days later, Malik stormed into the house.

'Did you remix our songs?' he demanded.

'Why?' Tara asked.

'A talent scout has got in touch,' Malik said.

'That's great news!' Tara said.

'Not for us, it isn't!' Malik said. 'He heard us play at the youth club and saw the video you put on YouTube. He says you're a genius and wants *you* to work for him.'

Tara drove Malik and the band to the recording studio. She insisted on talking to the talent scout.

'It's good to meet you,' the scout said, shaking Tara's hand. 'I was impressed with your skills. I want you to work your magic on some of my bands.'

'Only if you sign my brother and his band up, too,' Tara said.

The talent scout scratched his head. He thought for a few moments.

'OK,' he said. 'It's a deal! You're the one with the talent. But it's worth signing *them* just to get *you*!'

Curtain Call

alternative hip hop

audience

bling

breaking

creative

DJ Kool Herc

fashion

freeze

gig

gliding

graffiti

Grandmaster Flash
   and the Furious Five

jerking

jooking

locking

mixer

poetry

popping

rap

rapper

remix

rhythm

scratching

snapback

Snoop Dogg,
   Snoop Lion

talent

turntable

YouTube